INTRODUCTION

Love Astronomy or Astrology?

Then this adult coloring book is for you.
It features all the signs of the zodiac, the four elements,
the sun, the phases of the moon and the planets.

The Zodiac pages feature their element as the background image.
(Yes, Aquarius the Water Bearer is an AIR sign — go figure!)
The Element pages feature different variations
of those elements behind the alchemical symbols for each.
Just as the alchemical symbols for each of the planets
are laid out of a field of stars, and some feature
the day of the week that was named after them.

Each page is specifically designed to be one sided
so you don't have to worry about losing any artwork
if you want to take the pages out and frame them.
Also each page does not go to the edges
so that you can color over by the spine without any hassles!

You have my permission to photocopy the images for personal use only,
the Zodiac signs in particular make great gifts.

Whether you like to read horoscopes or stare up into the night sky,
this coloring book has something for all.

Art should be fun and relaxing, so go crazy!

Enjoy!
♥ Meredith

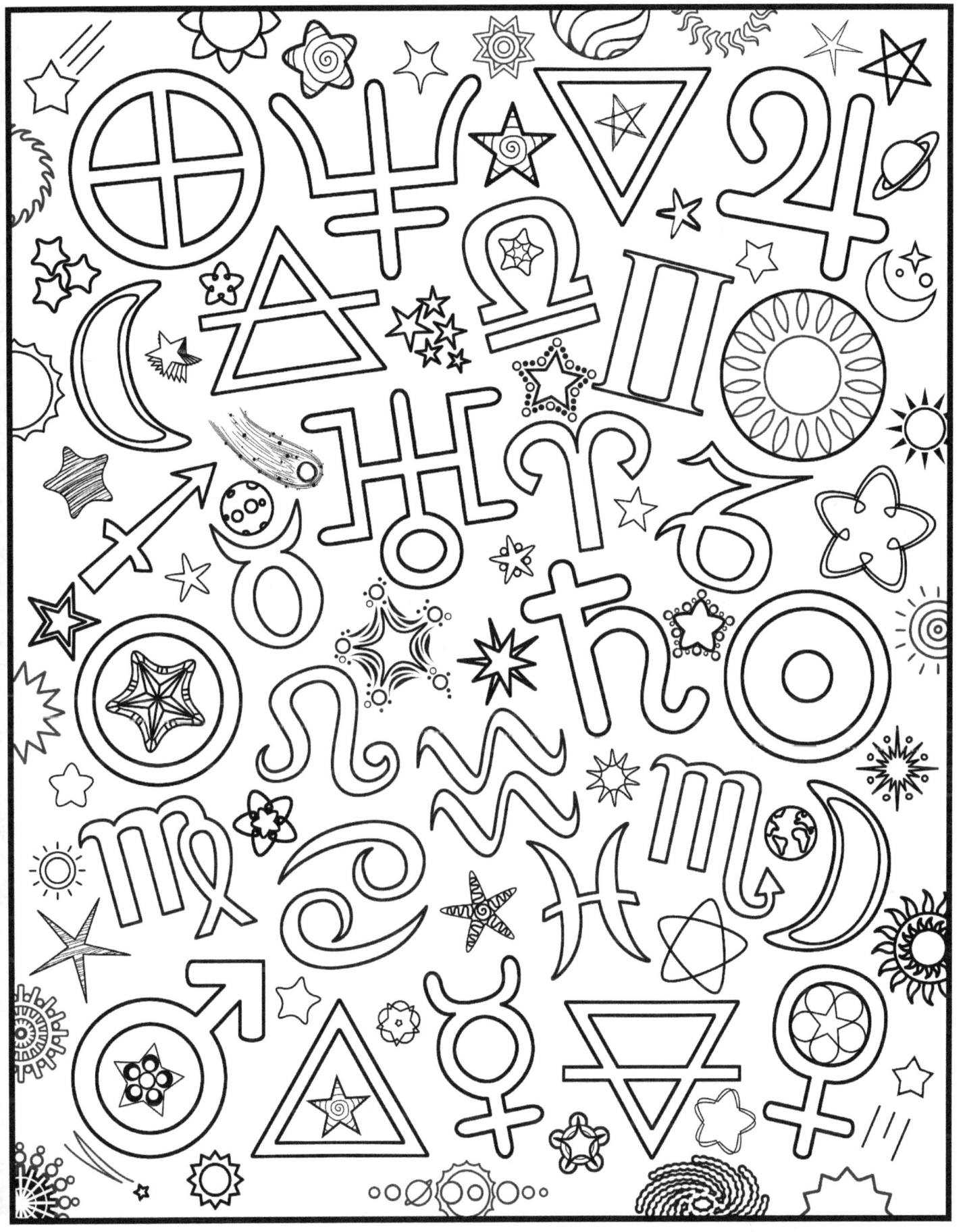

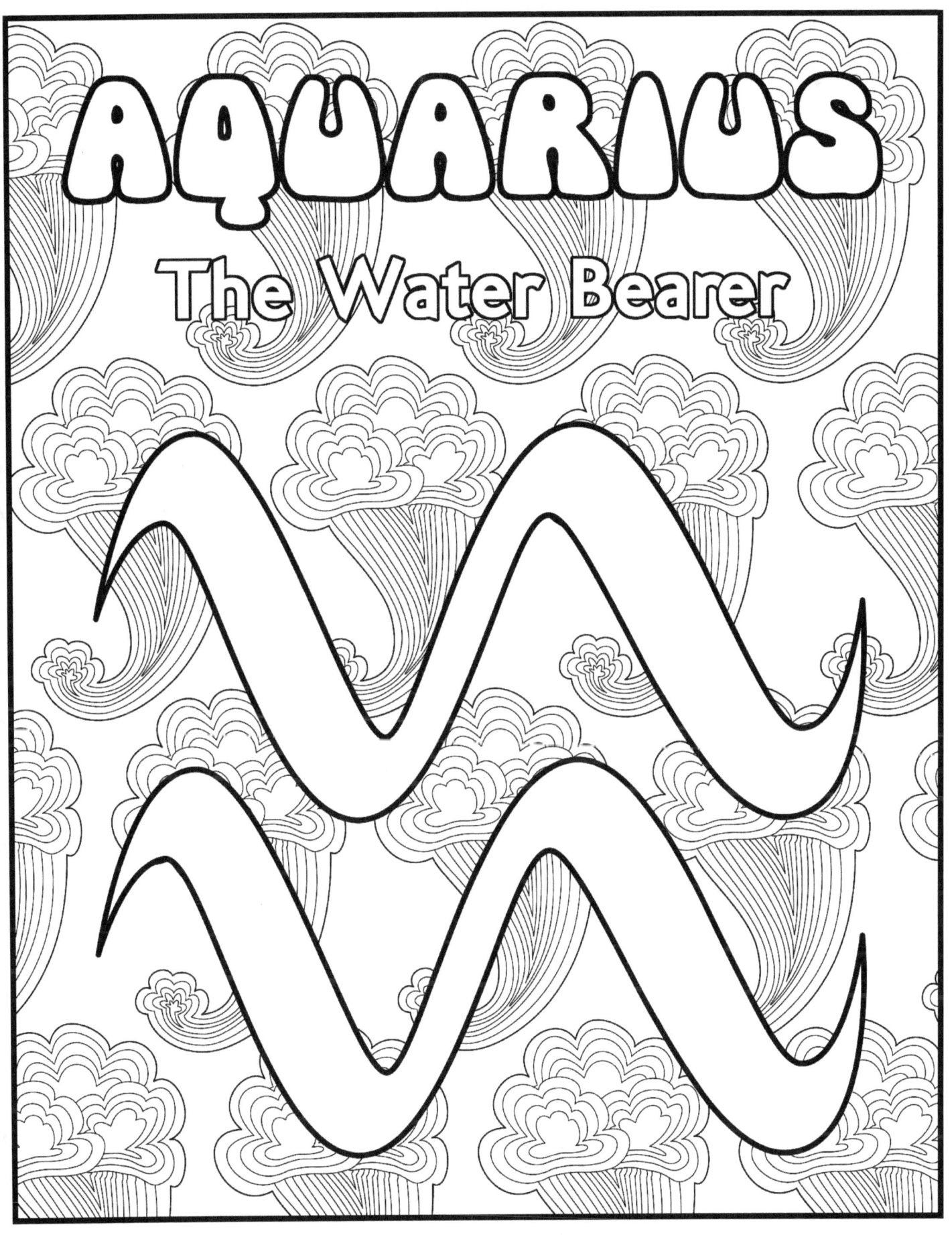

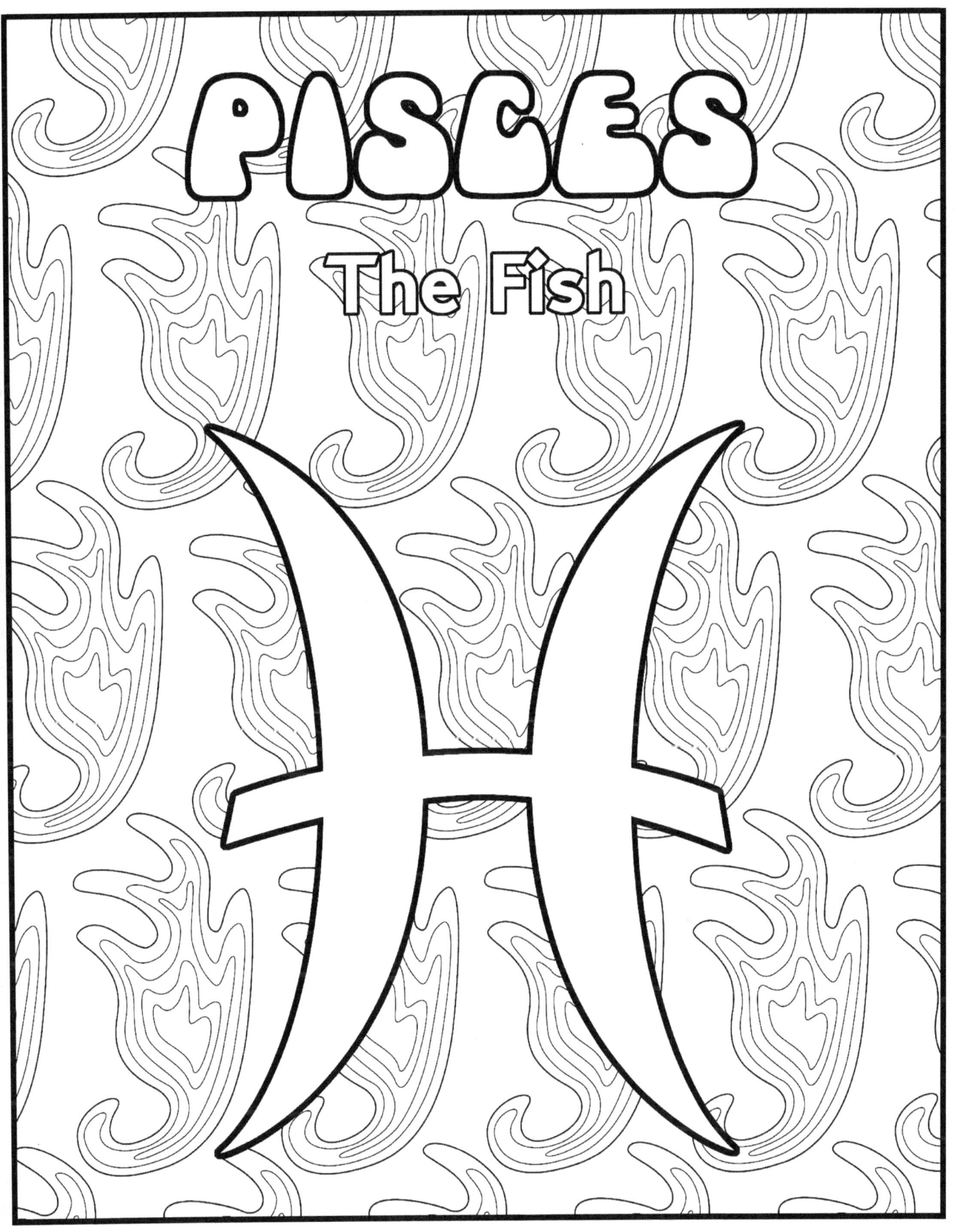

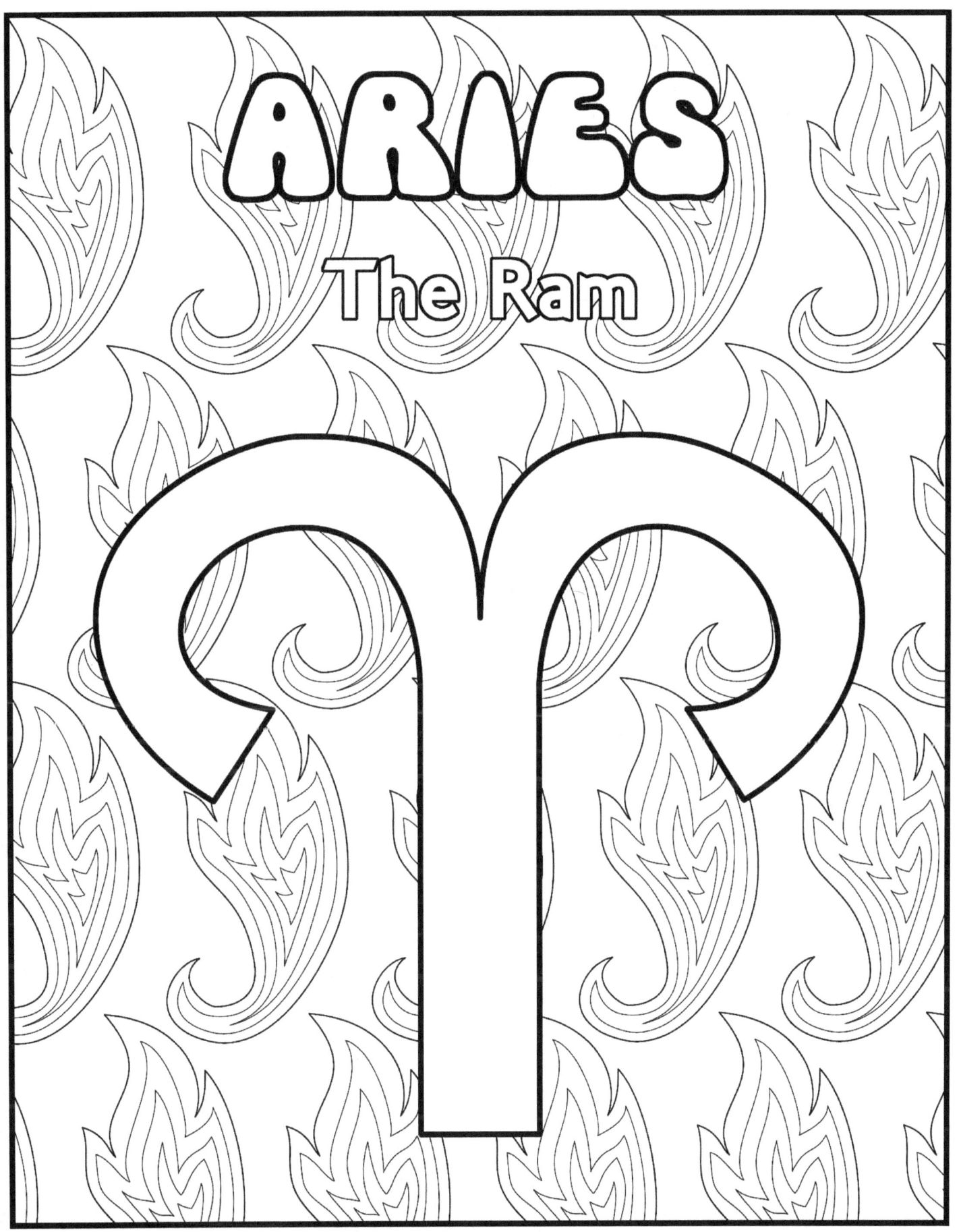

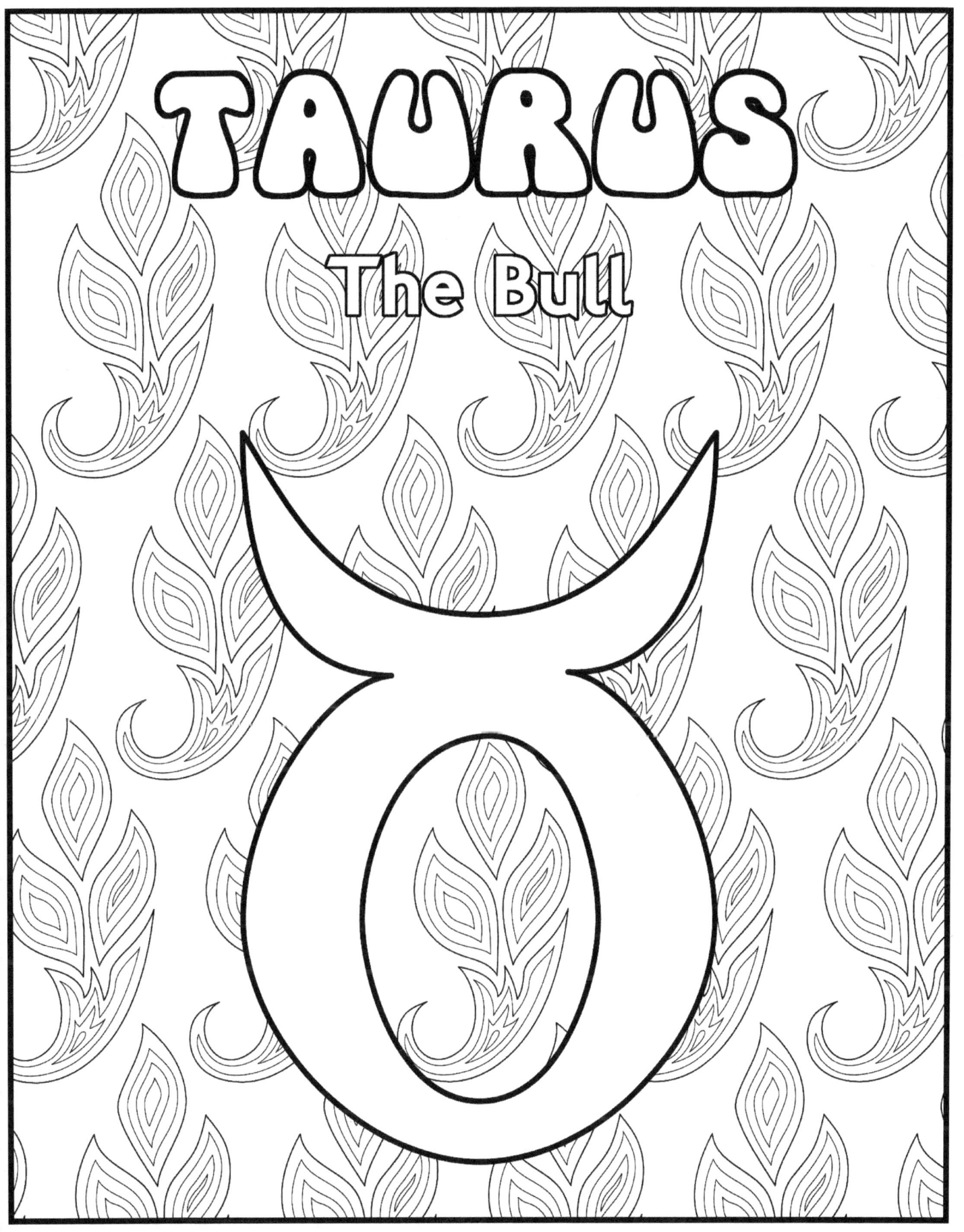

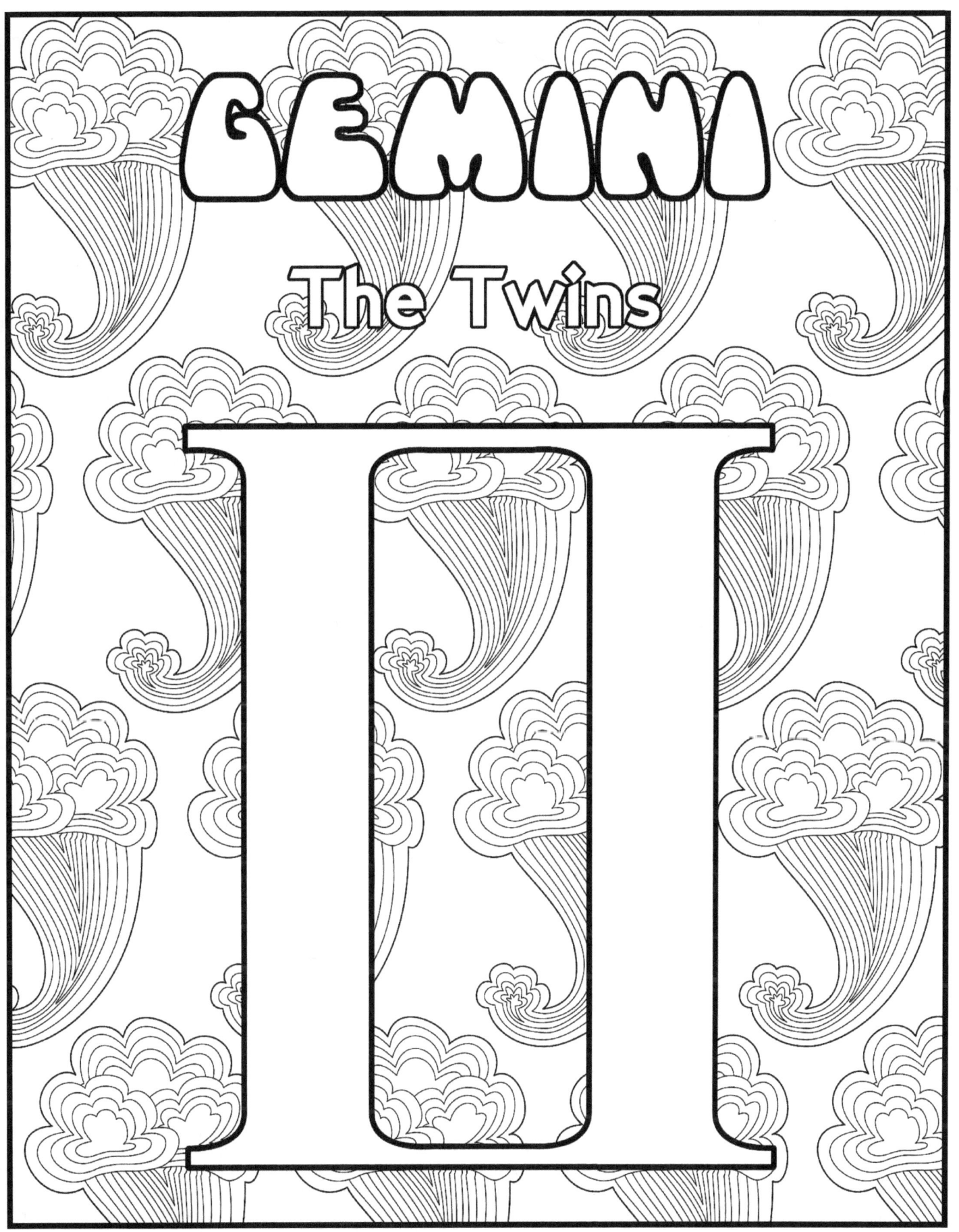

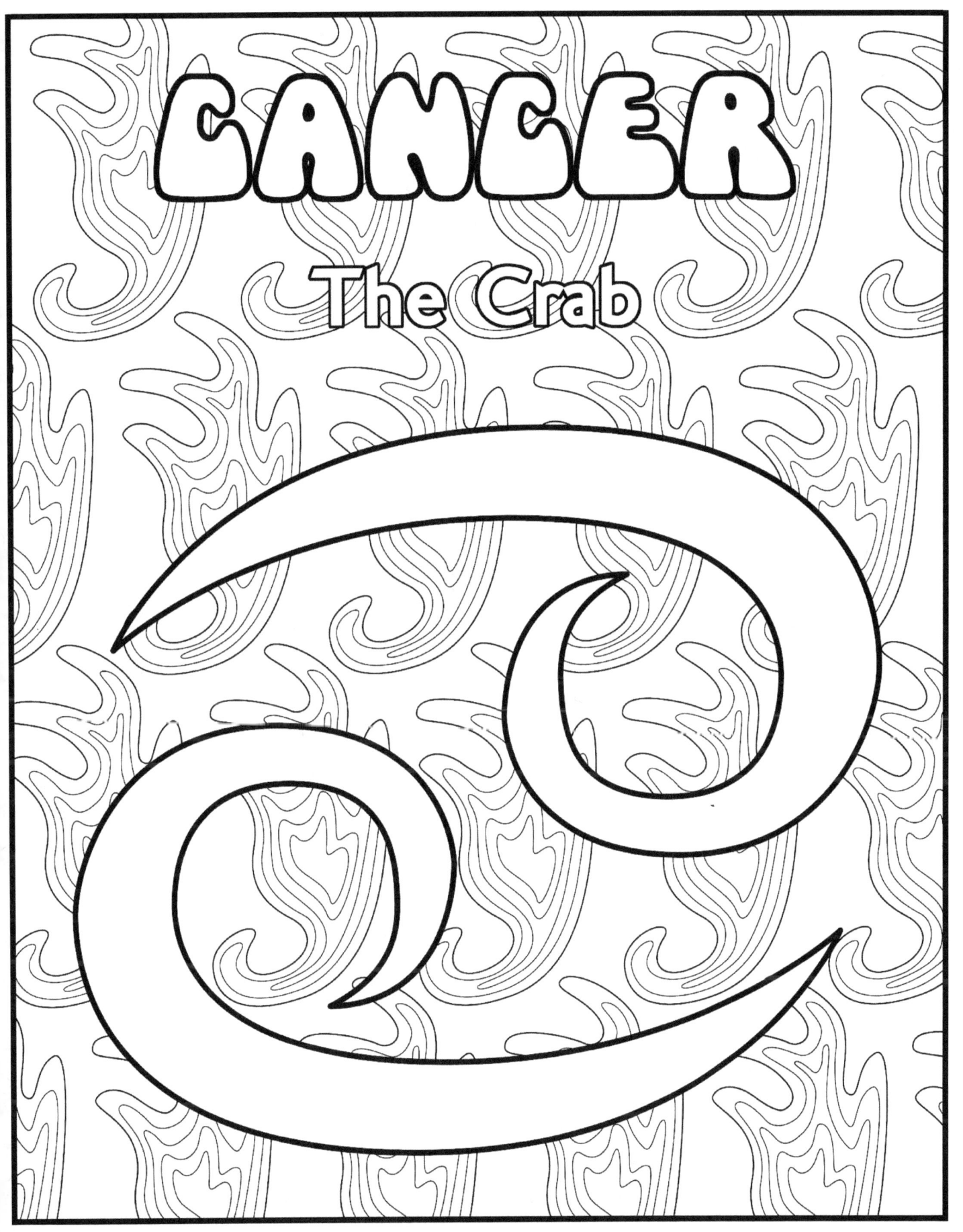

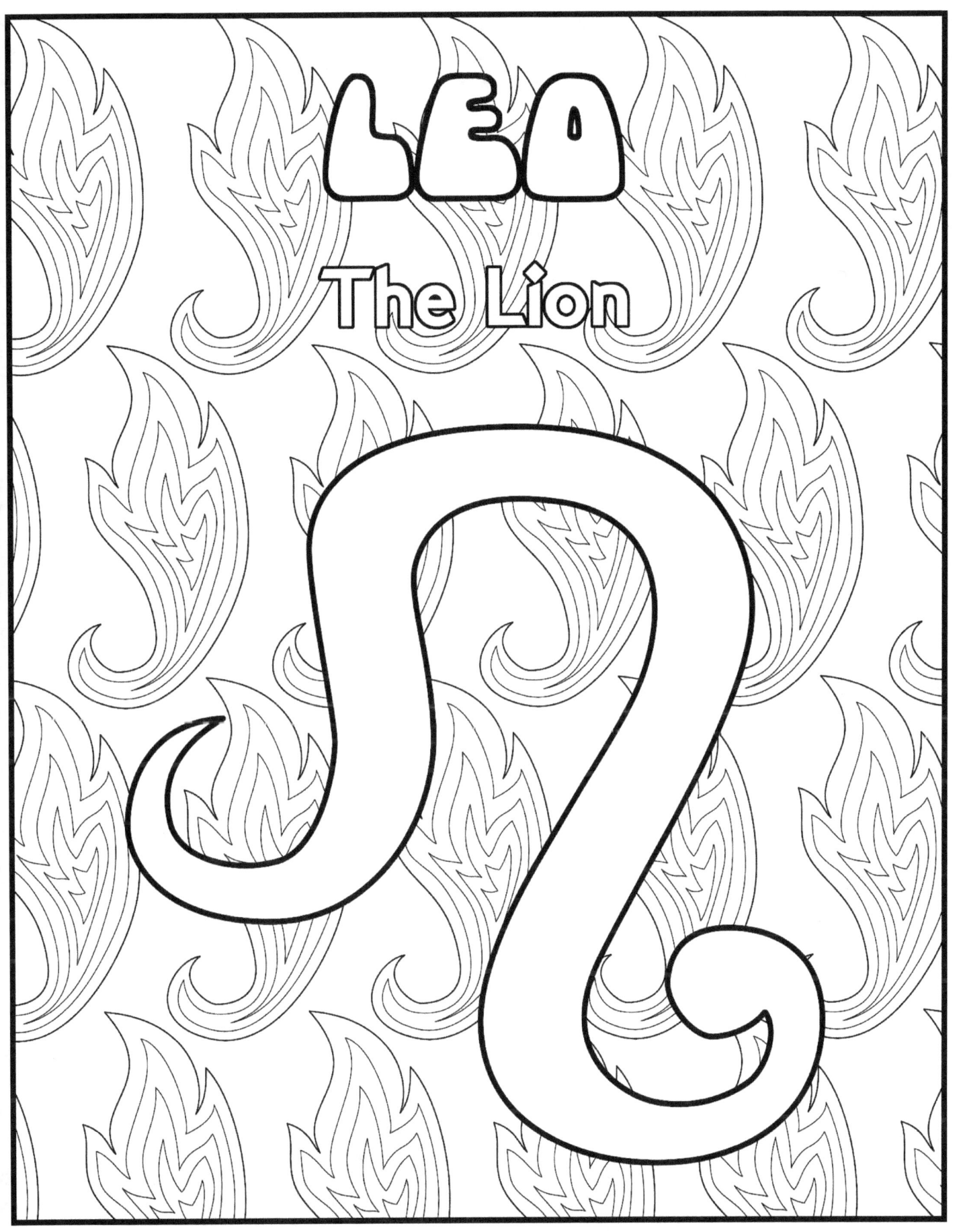

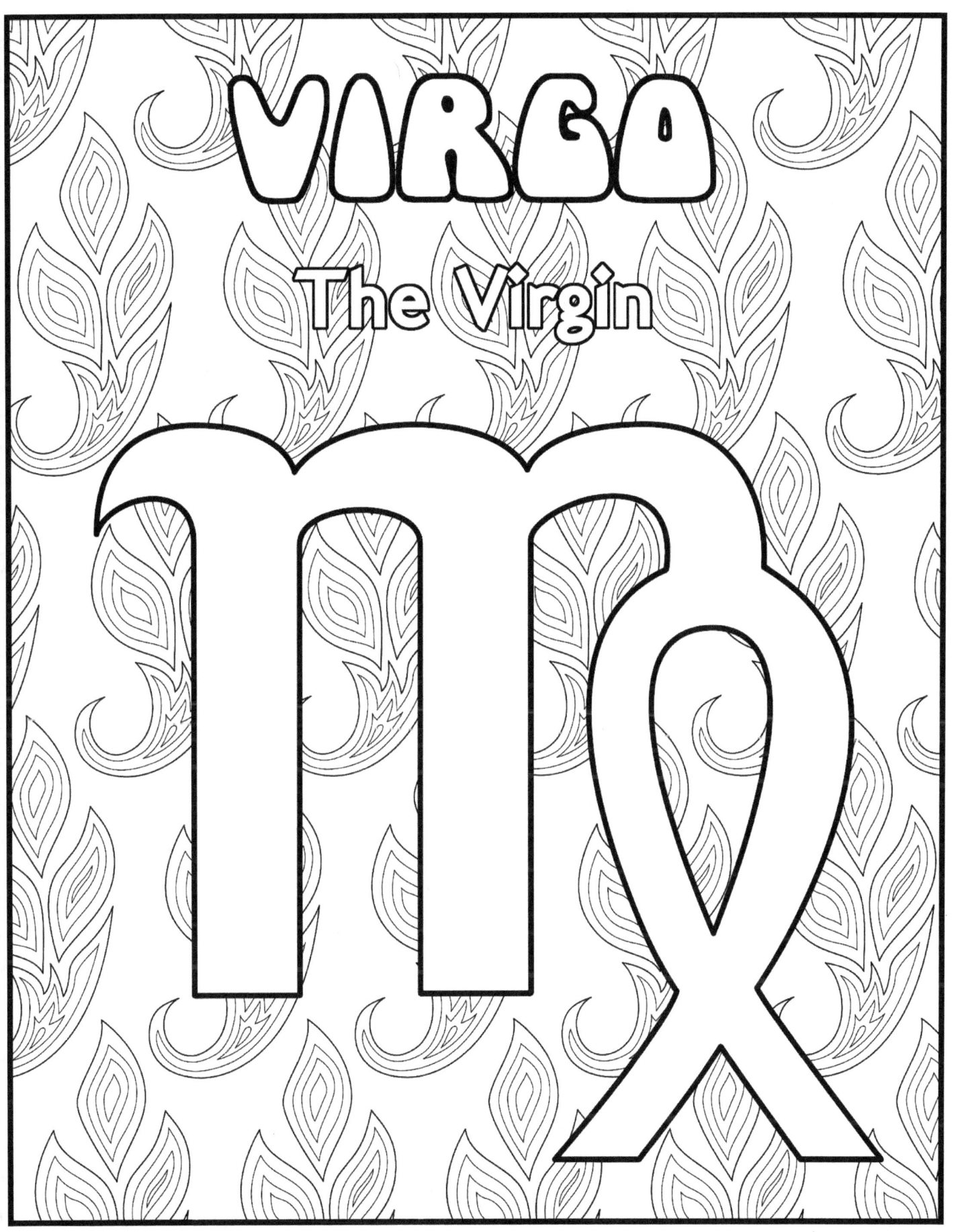

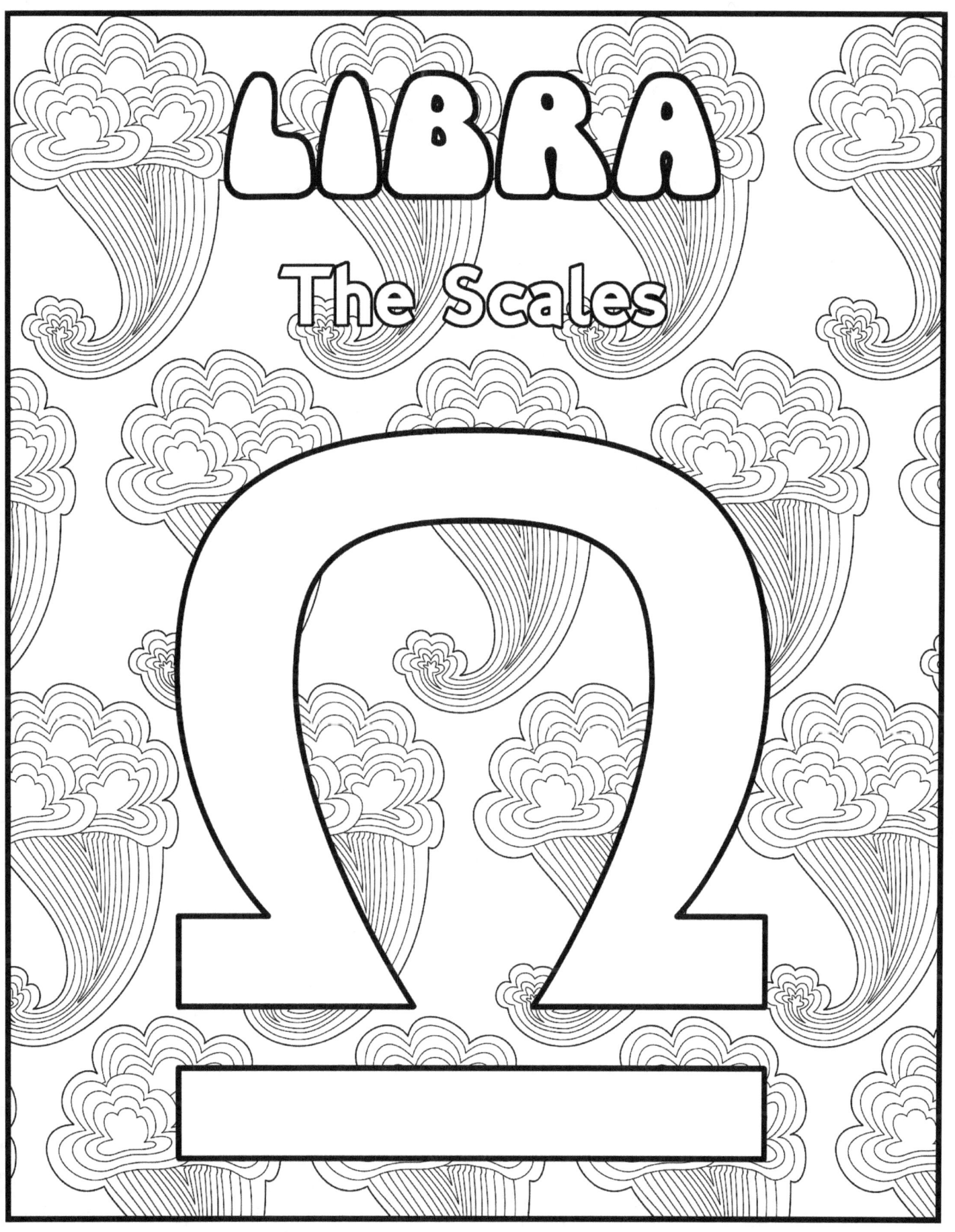

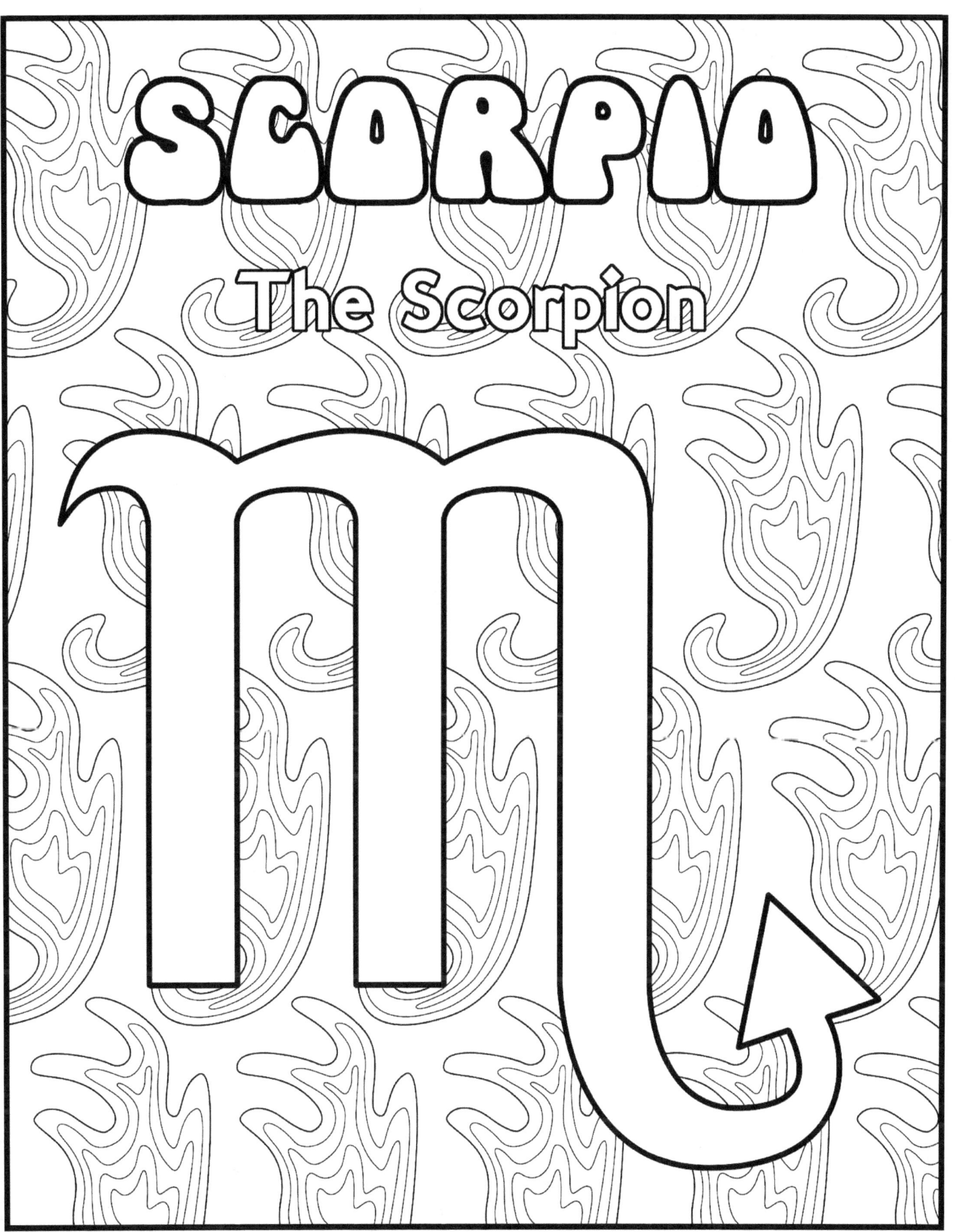

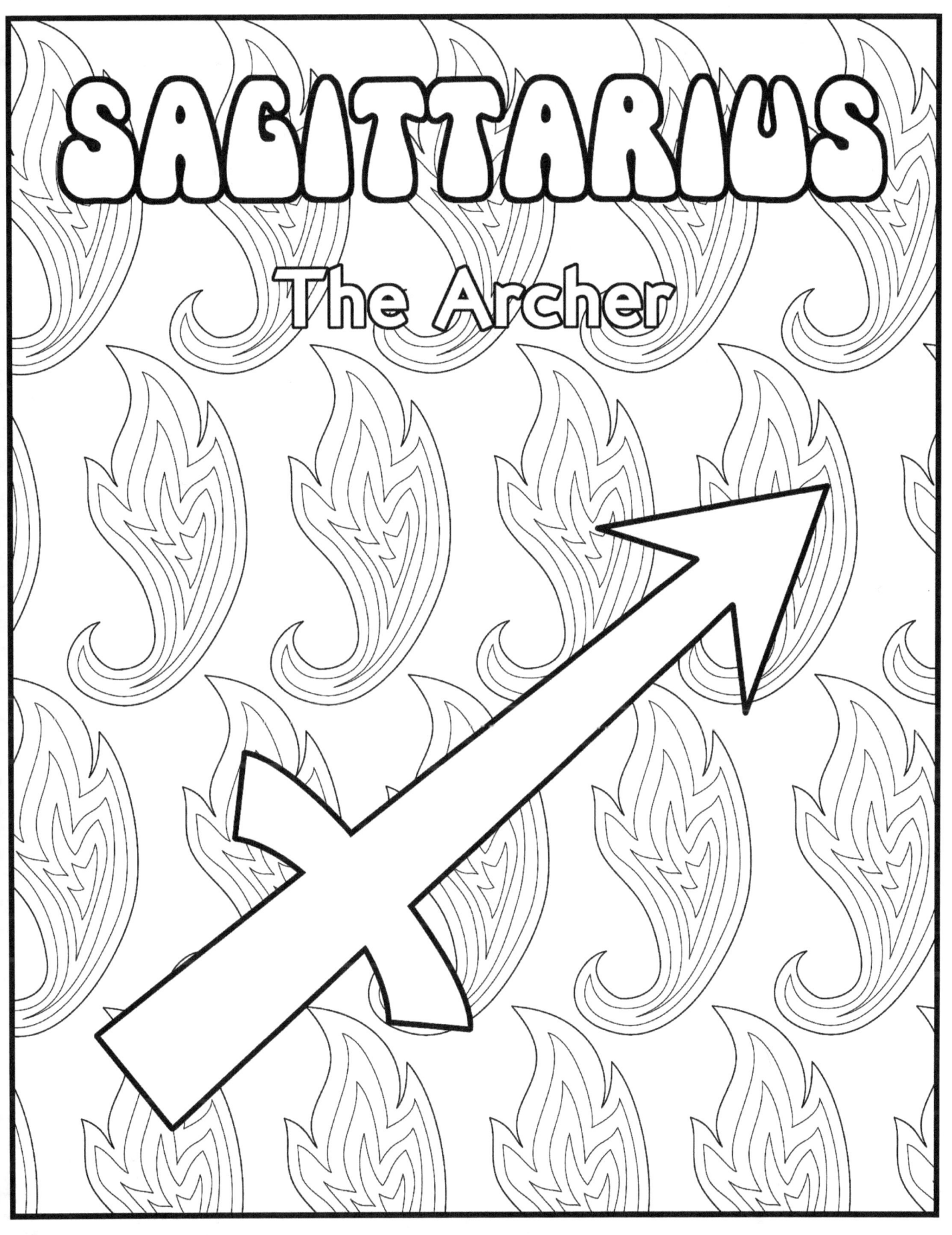

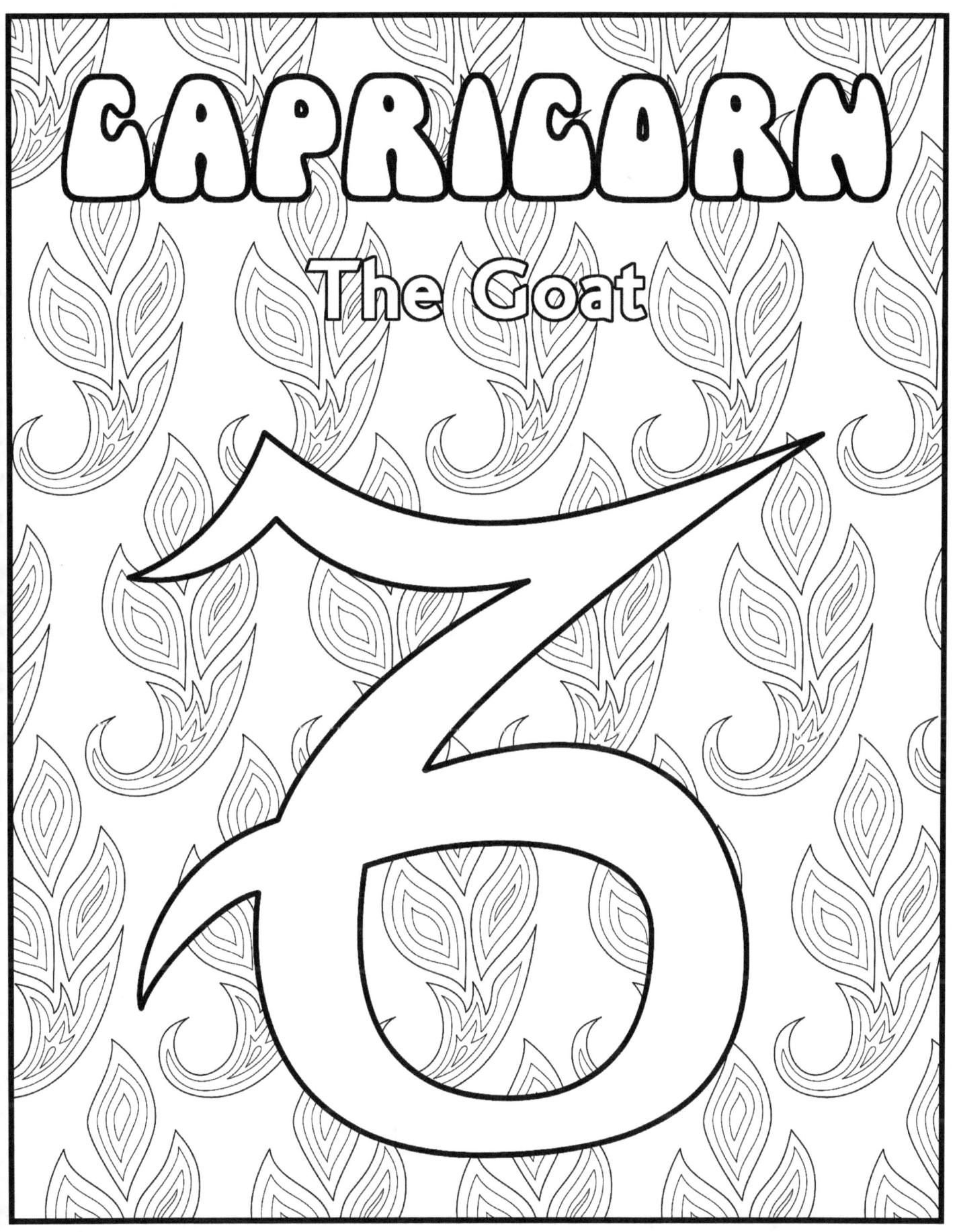

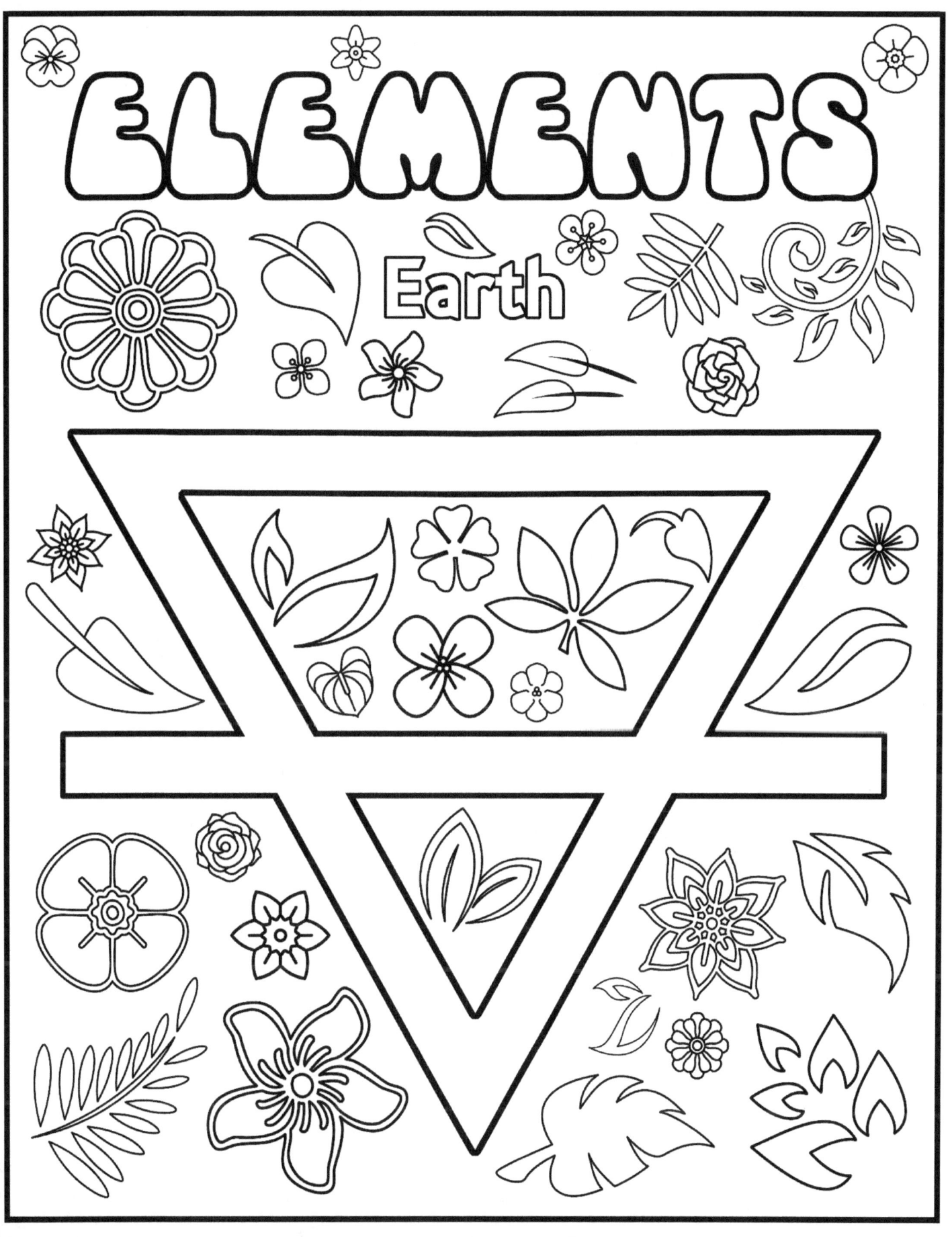

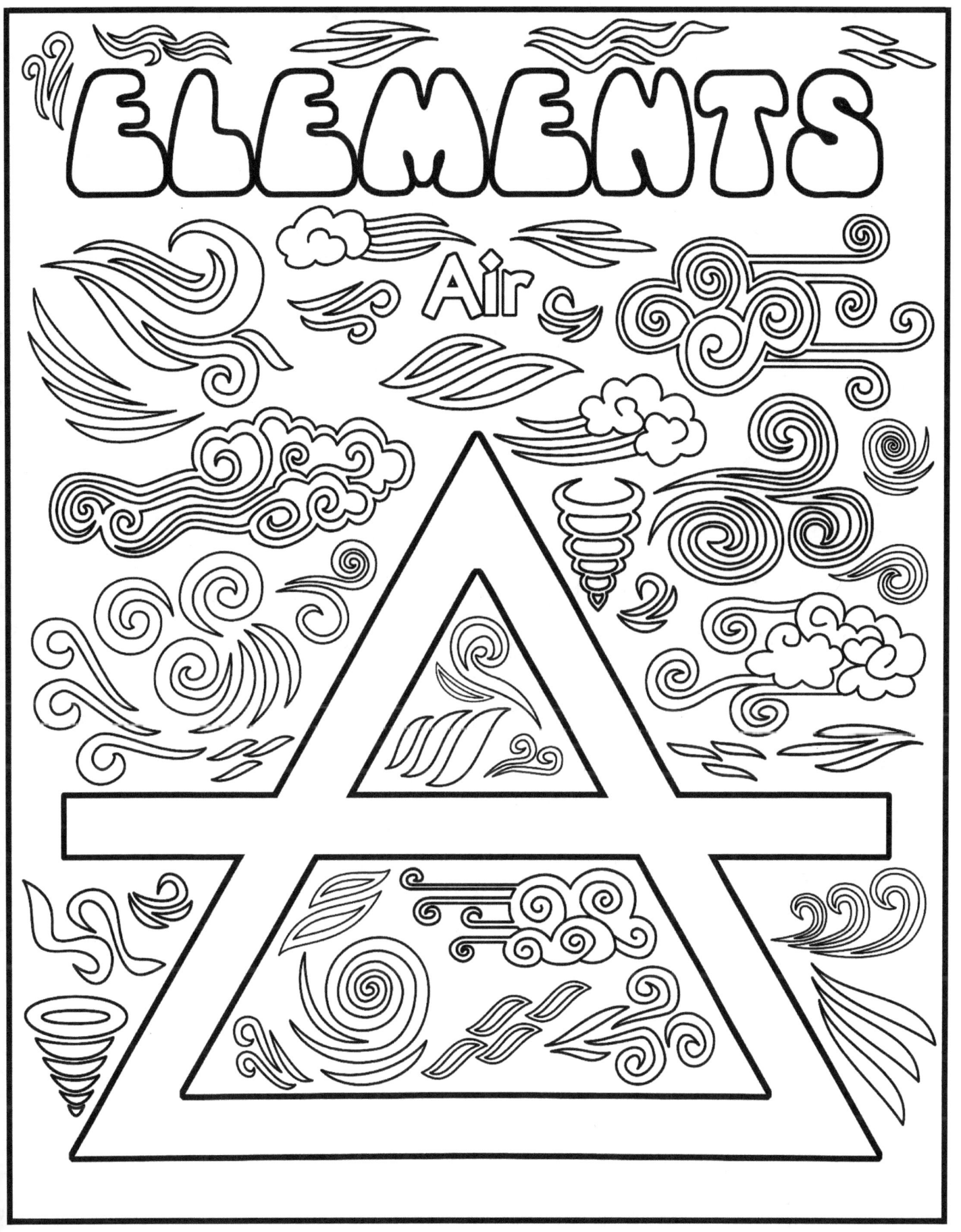

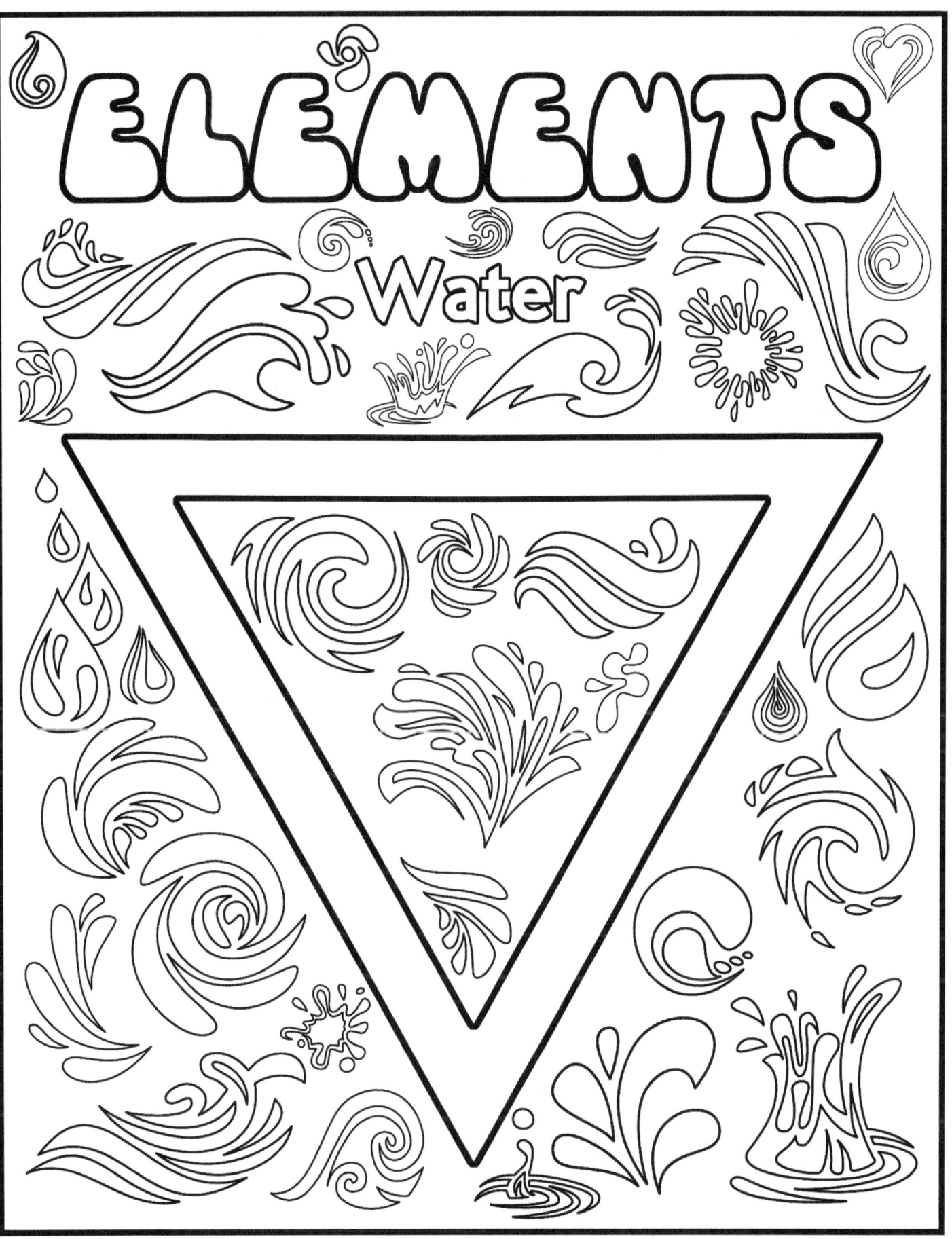

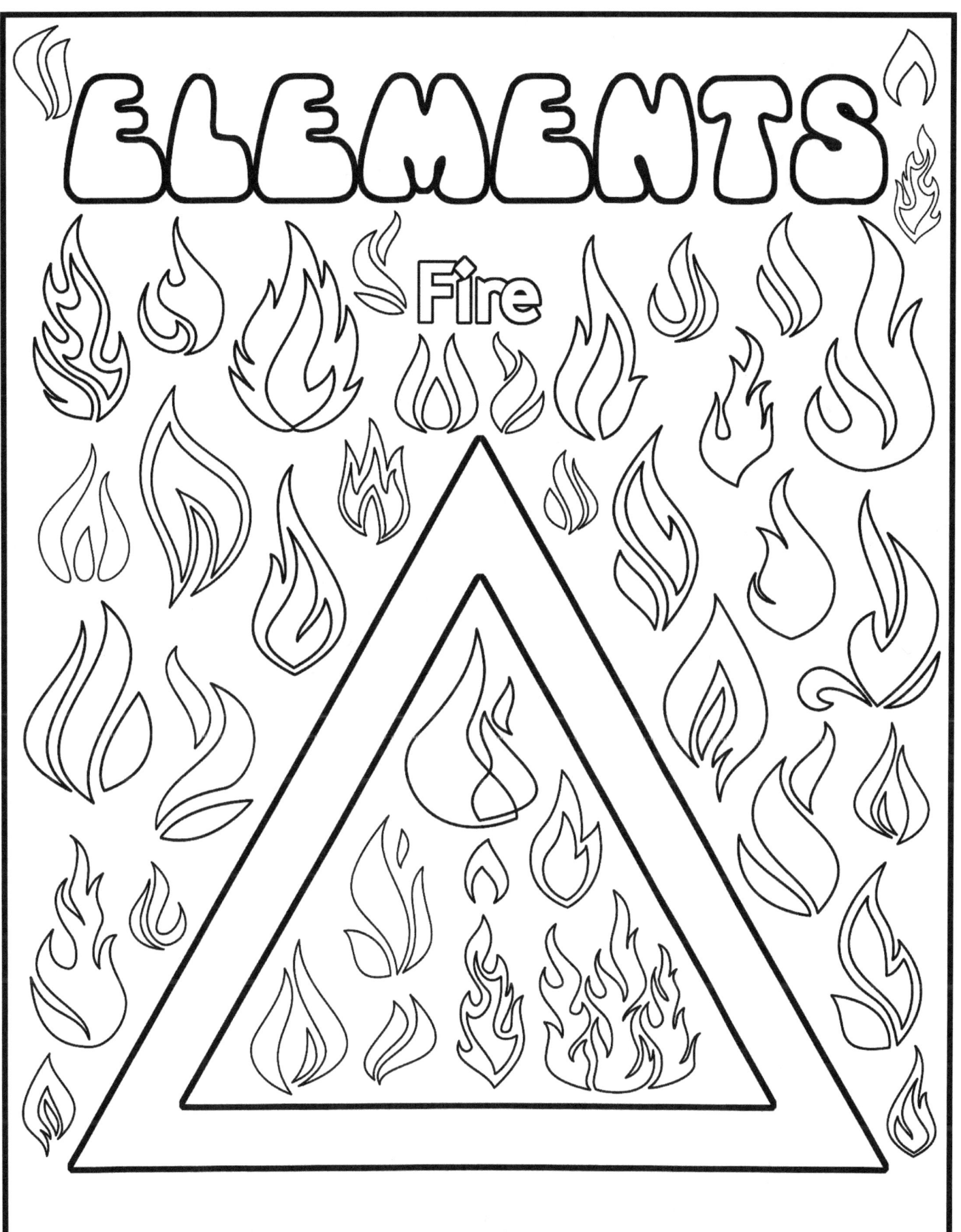

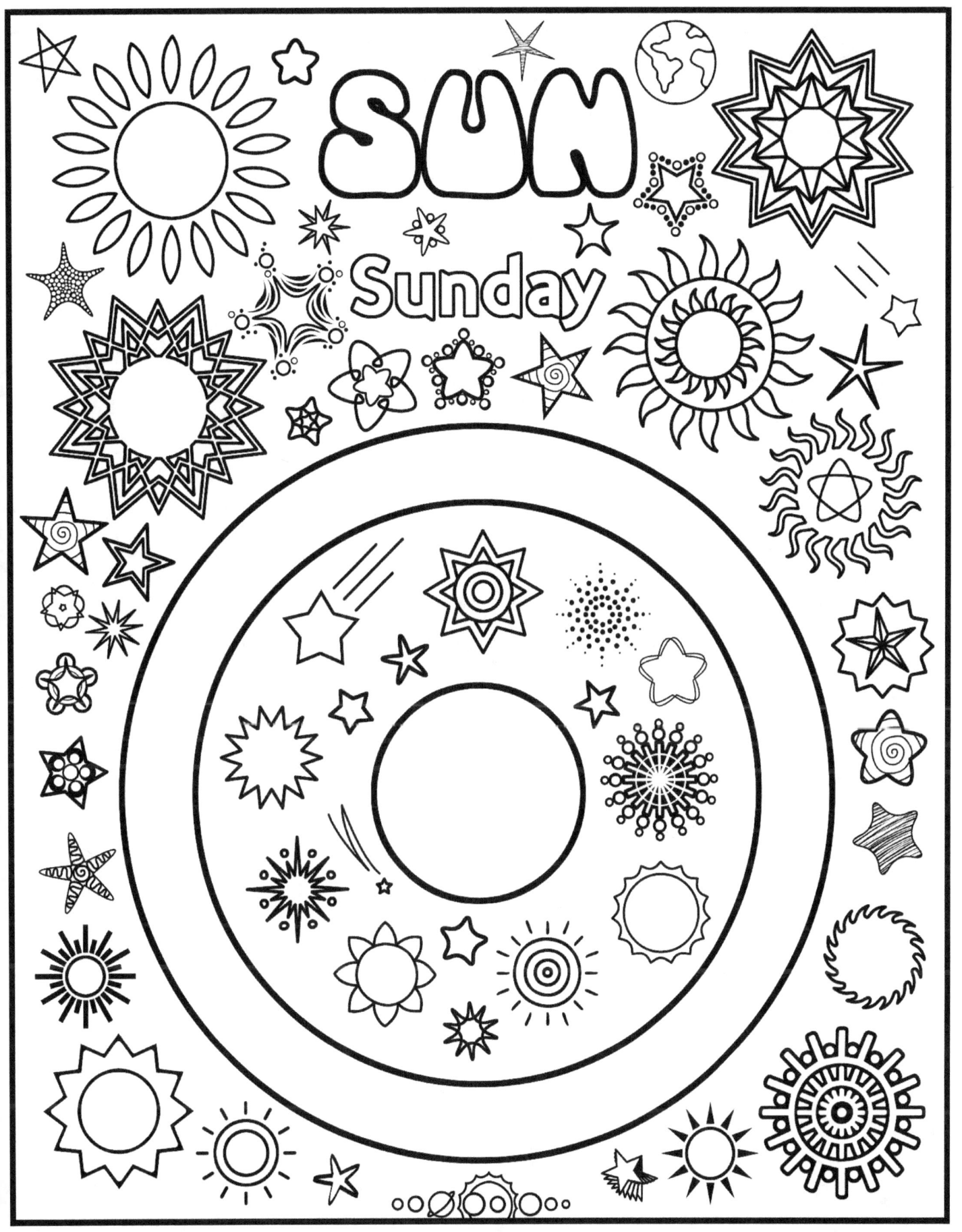

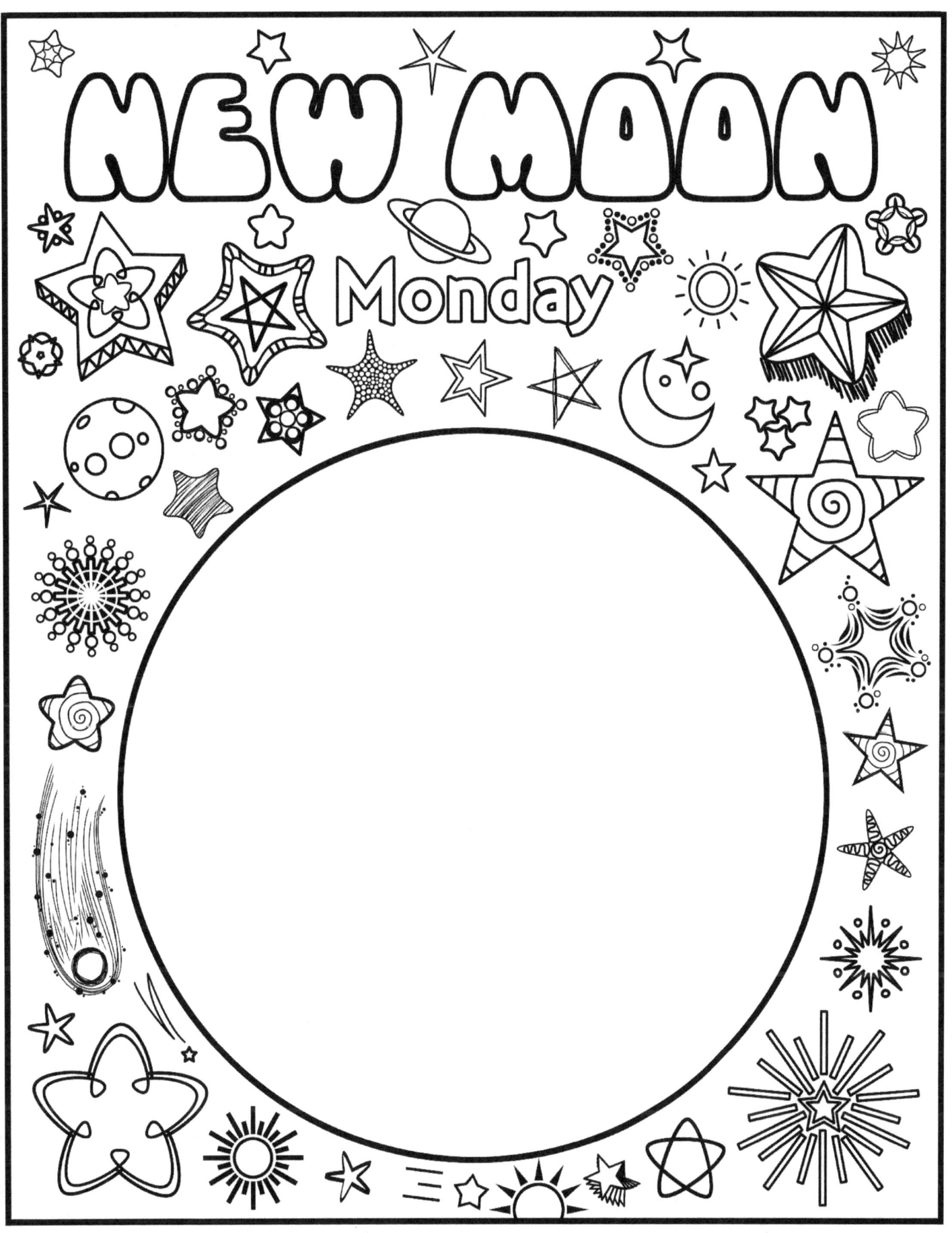

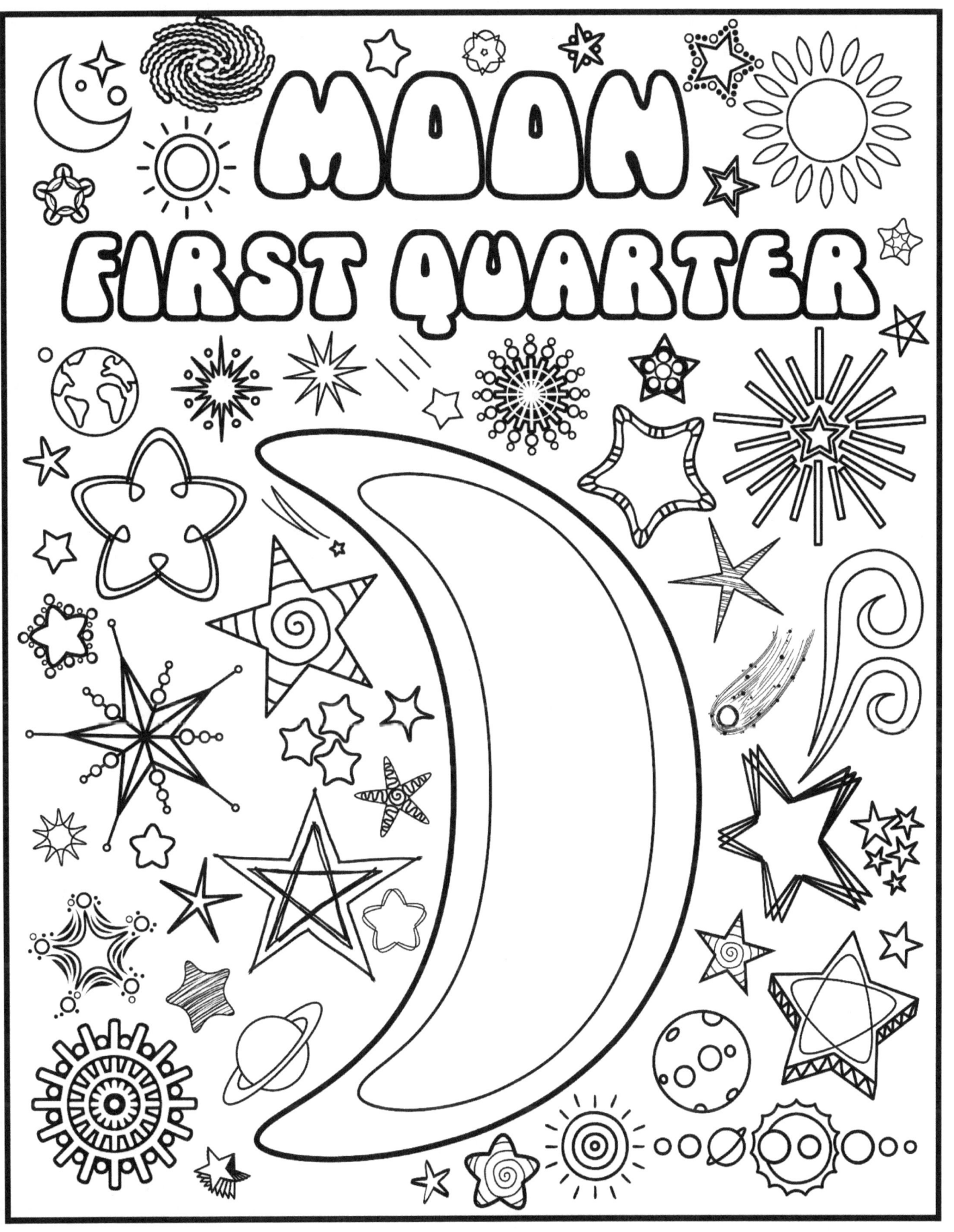

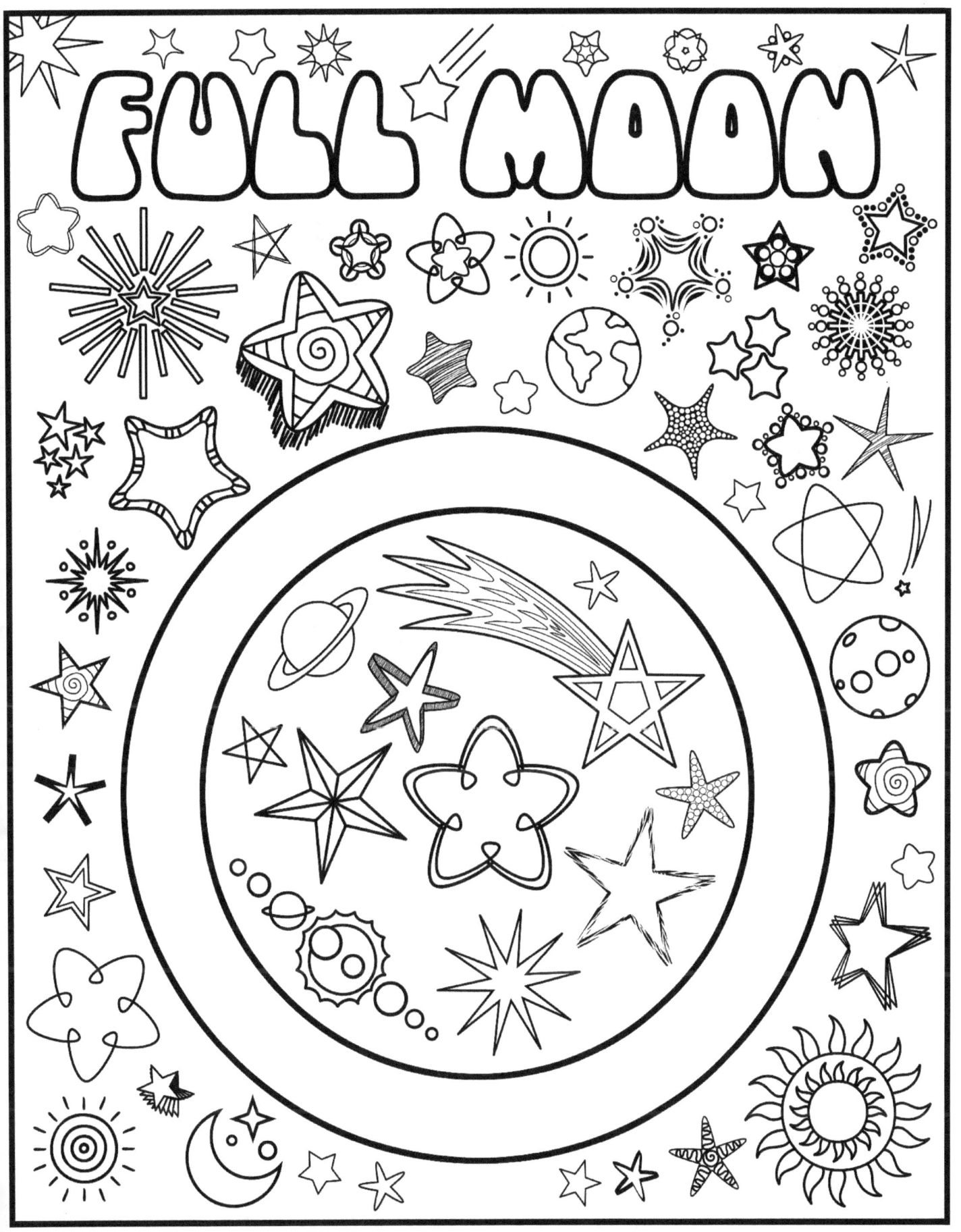

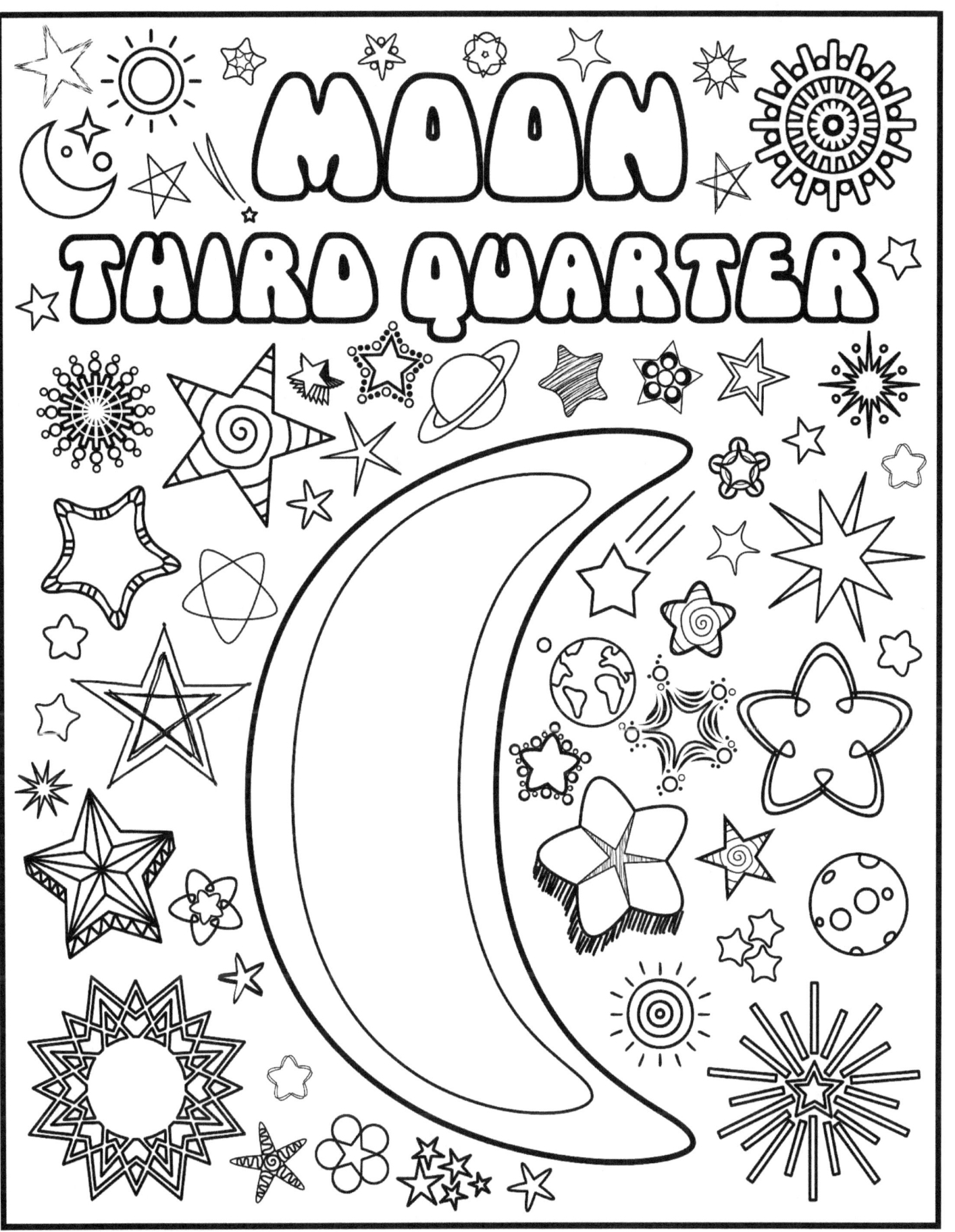

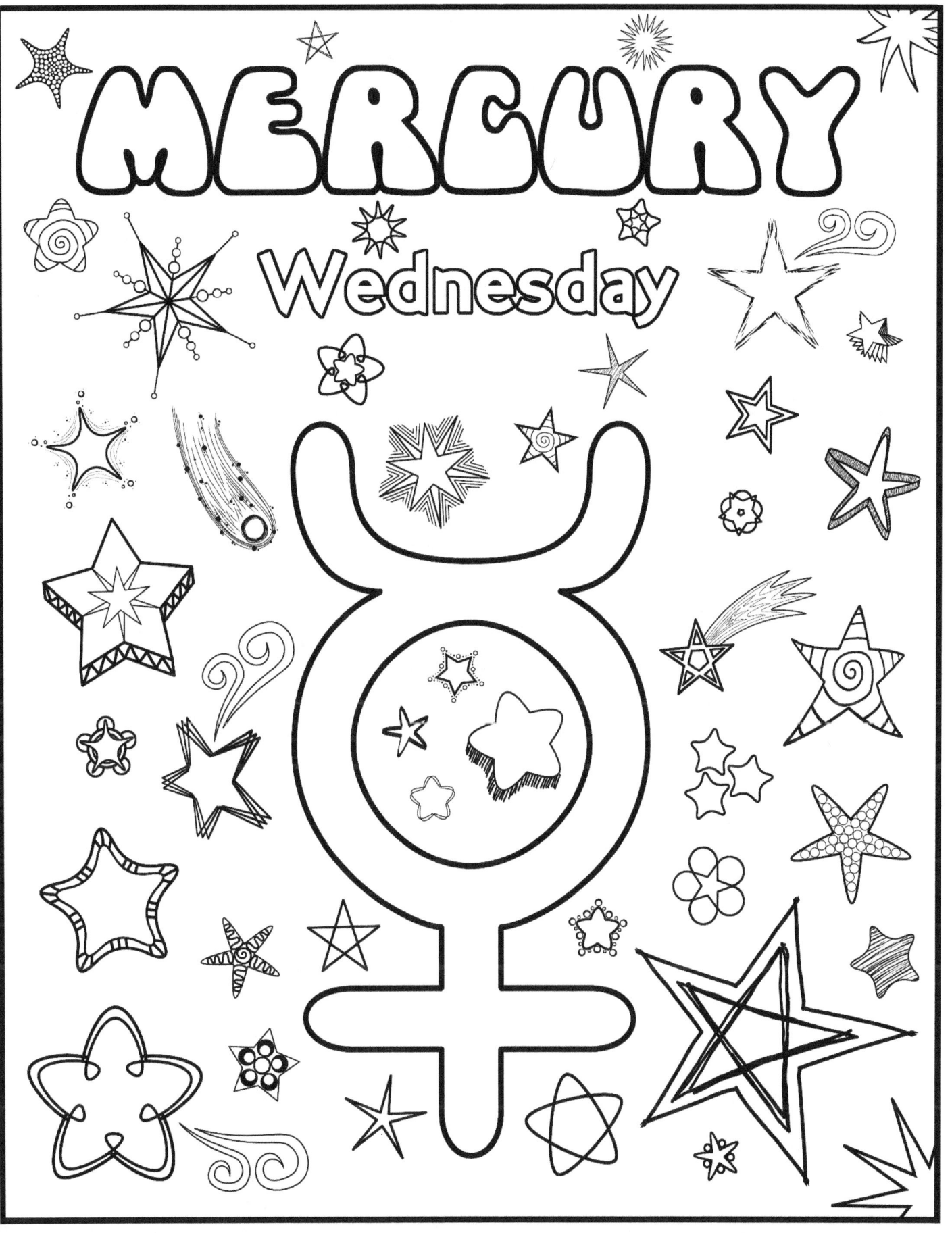

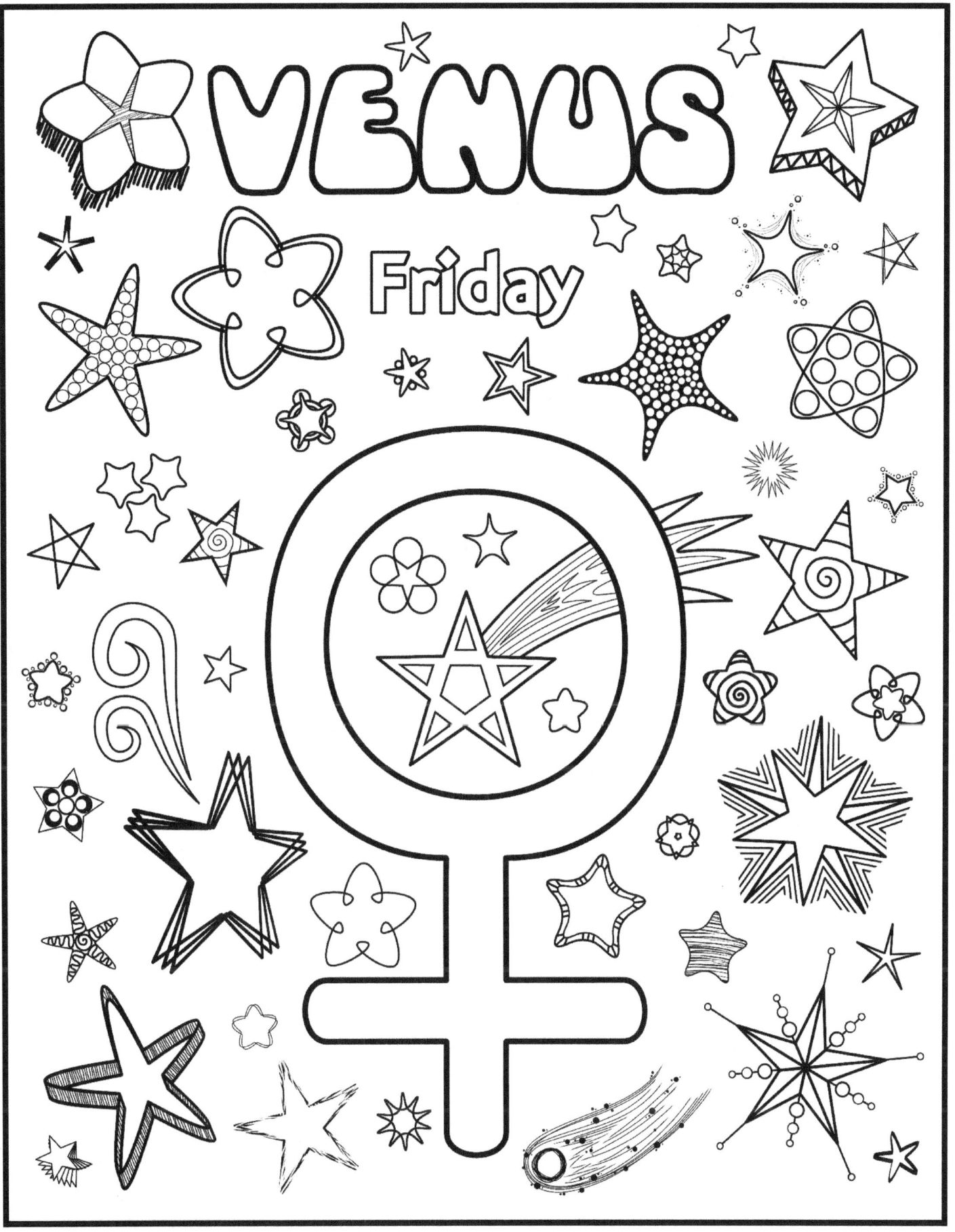

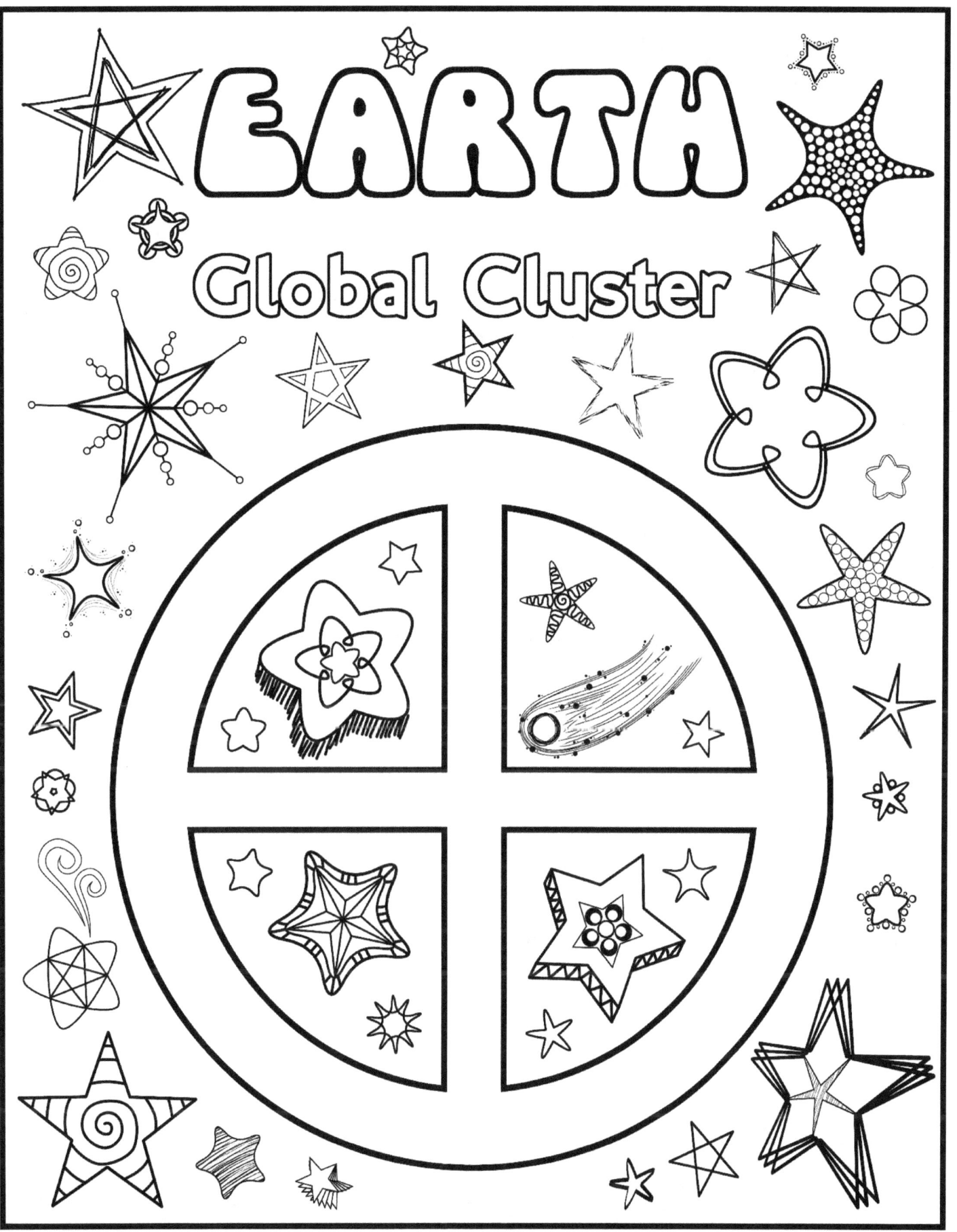

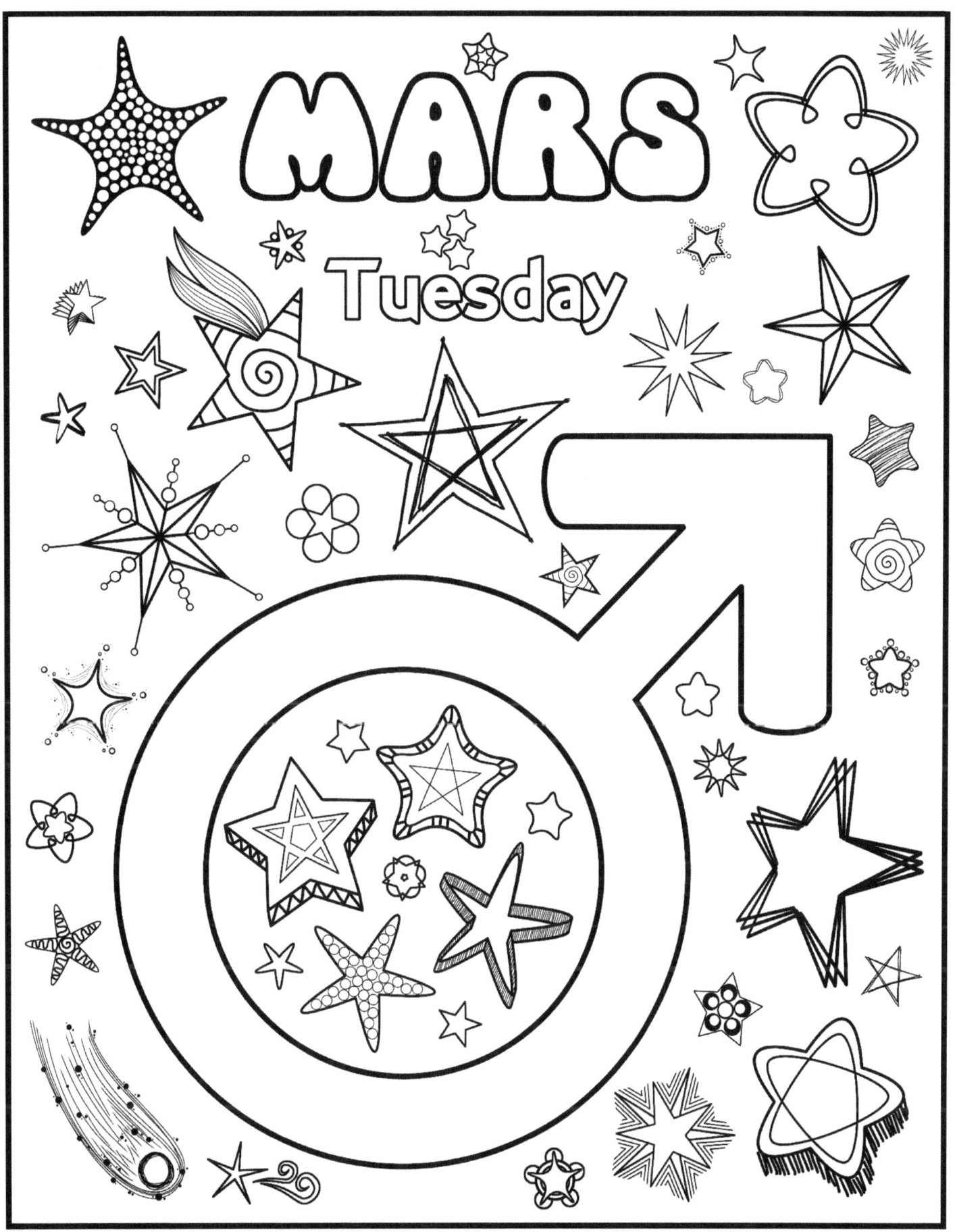

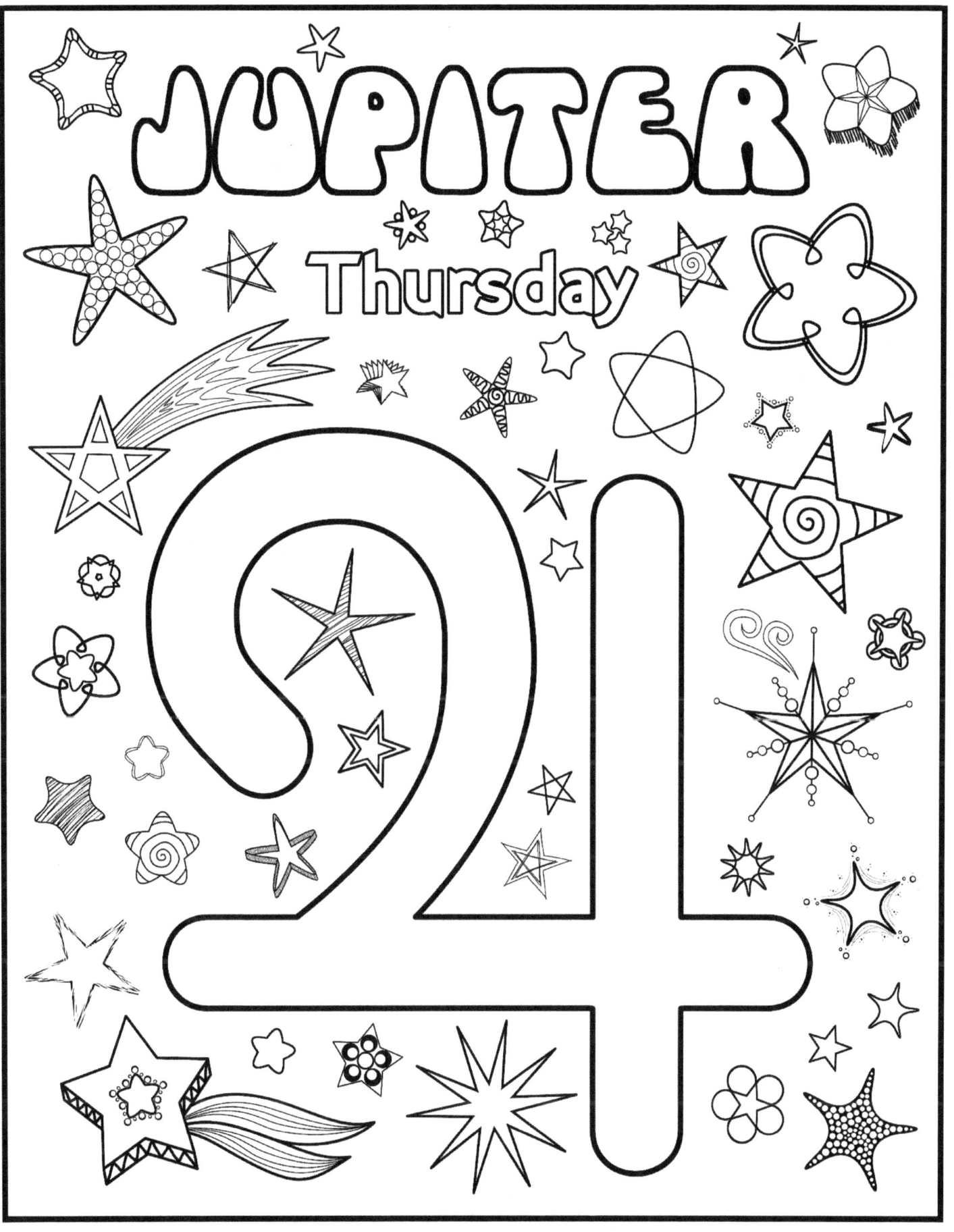

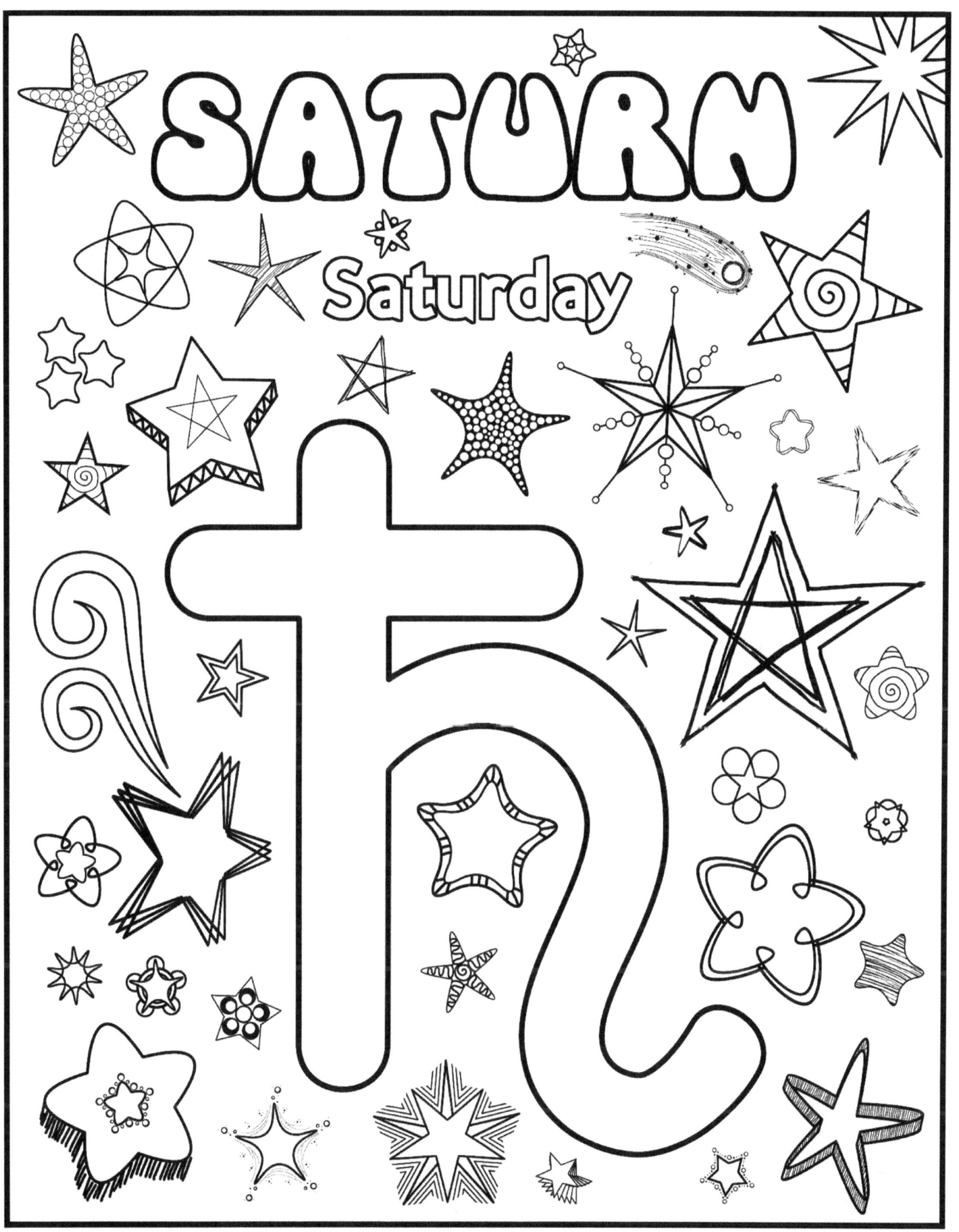

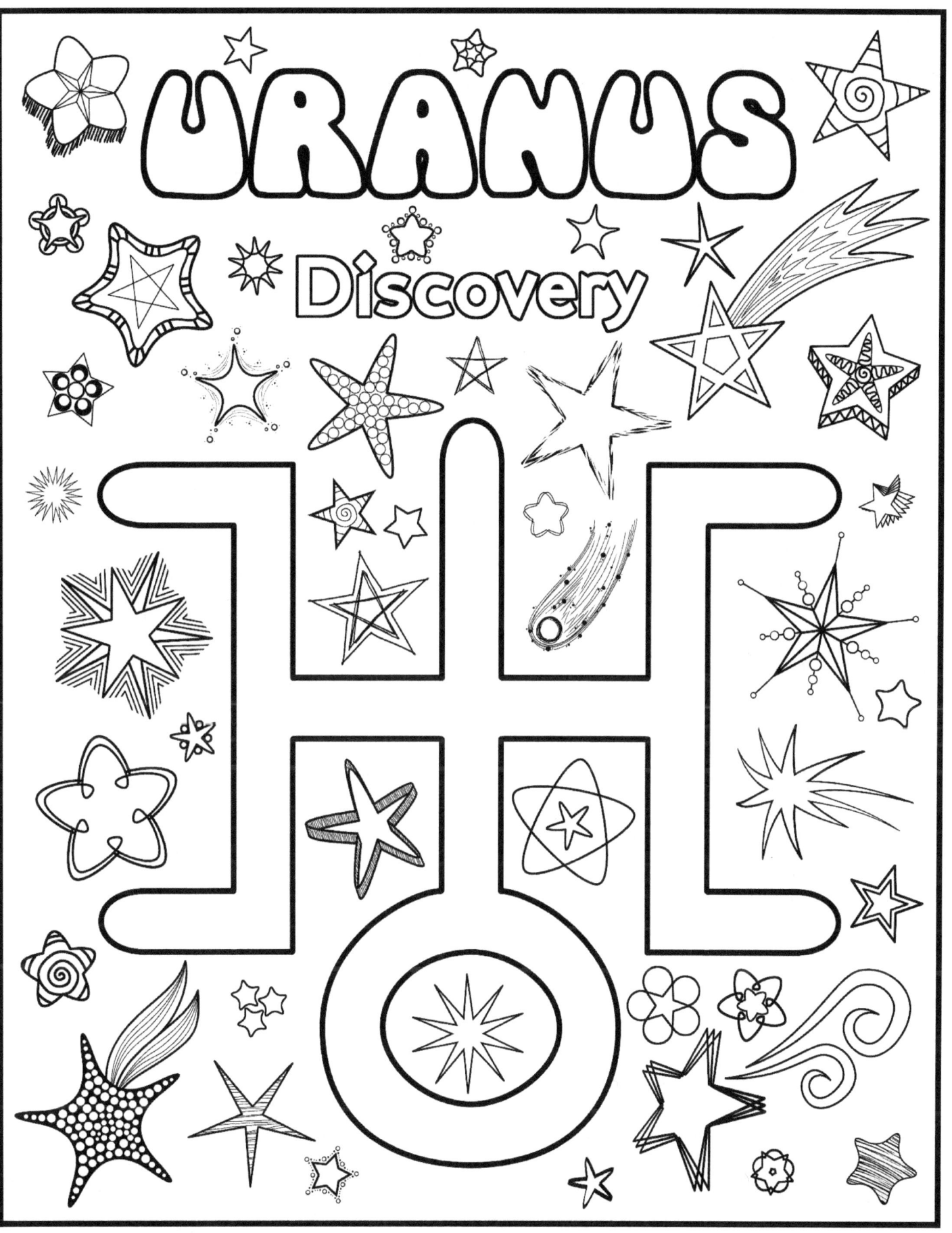

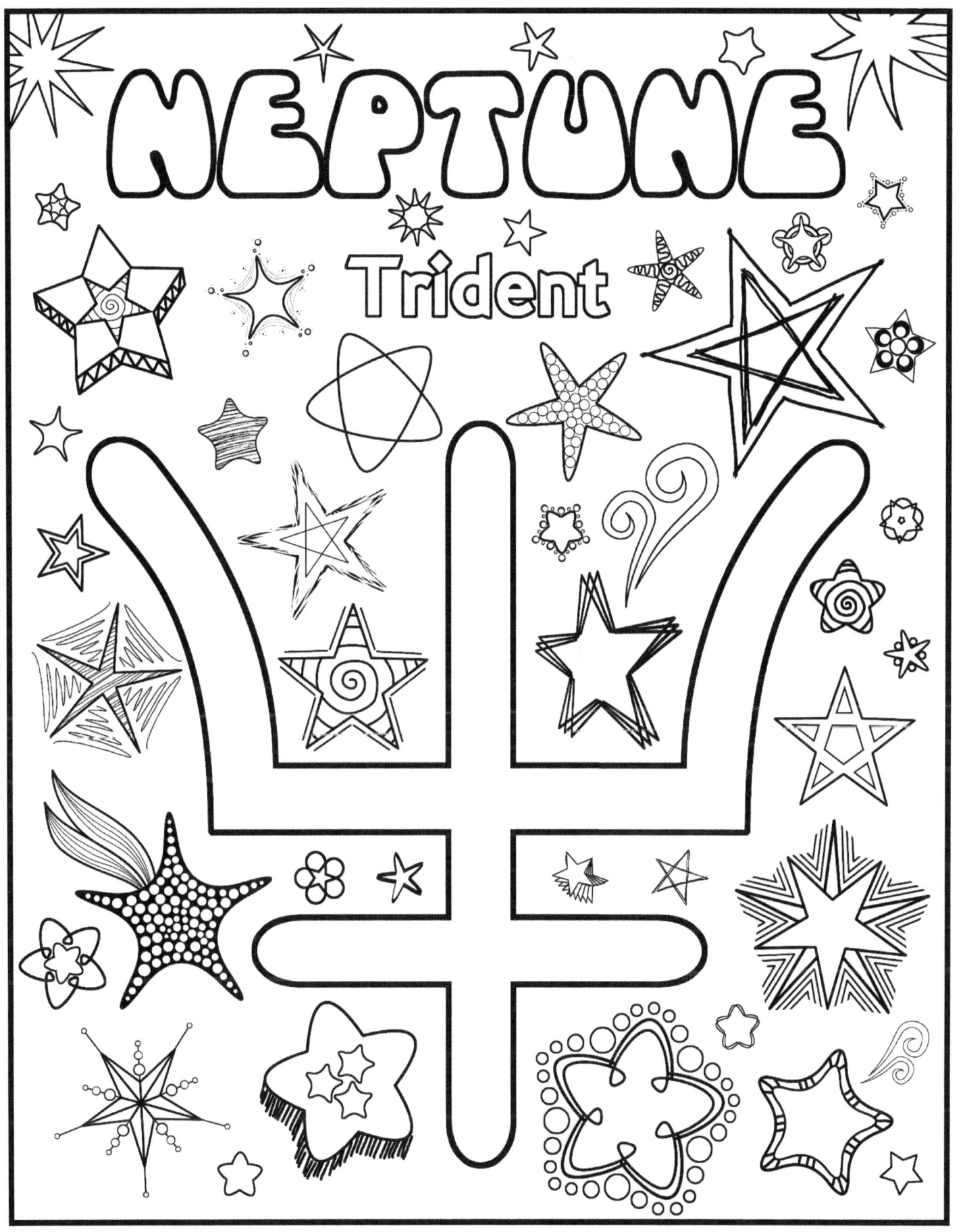

www.ingramcontent.com/pod-product-compliance
Lightning Source LLC
Chambersburg PA
CBHW062157220526
45470CB00009B/2853